Harp of the
ONE HEART

John G Ryan

ISBN: **098814834X**
ISBN-13**: 978-0988148345**

Harp
Of

The One Heart

You are about to embark on a journey
into a vista where the love of life has
not been twisted into contortions of
fear or forgetfulness.

Allow the vibrations of these sacred
songs and images to touch deep into
your memory, for this vista is none
other than a memory of the future
which lies dormant and ready to
blossom in the heart of mankind.

I ask you make space to enjoy them in
a way that truly caresses you ... in a
way only you may know and you truly
deserve ...

ECHOES OF THE HARP

ACKNOWLEDGEMENTS

To the light that lay dormant in the bud of
humanity …
The wisdom that makes our world a better place …
And the love within each of us to share.

I

HARP
OF THE
ONE HEART

harp of the One Heart

My heart does long for tender days,
Where breezes of sweet nature's ways,
Caress the woes of saddened dreams,
To wash away in earthly streams.

My body longs for lively rest,
Where dreams anew flow through my breast.
Sacred solace spinning anew,
A sacred dream does long flow through.

Remember a future release a past,
Whose sorrow's crafted sea skilled mast,
Rides weathered boat by storms intent,
Into a dawn storms want prevent.

Turbulence of ill wrought streams,
Calm by decrees of my sweet dreams.
Raise high the hopes of destined sail,
My dream, my love it shall prevail.

Harp of the One Heart

Look not upon the scars which fade,

Look brightly to the promise made,

To life's seeds of tree divine,

Which flourish through the mists sublime.

Pour forth the light to burn anew.

Passion in my breast is You.

Illumine sparks of Your desire,

Hearts dreams aglow - celestial fire.

I shall not succumb to illusions ways.

My life now flows upon your rays.

No shadow dare to caste a dream,

That veils the life upon that stream.

Living praise my heart now sings.

Voice of the choirs in cosmos rings.

Harp of the One Heart call your muse,

My heart once mine is Yours to use.

Call

I call to the angels for mercy and peace
To sooth o'er the wounds
That my company keep.

I call to the angels for grace on the land
Whose torments and fragments
Are brought forth through man.

I call to the angels for kindness in heart
As the cries of earth's people
Call a new world to start.

I call to the angels for wisdom of being
To clear fear's illusion
From man's way of seeing.

I call to the angels the humble to rise

To birth forth the sacred

a flame in our eyes.

I call forth the angels to make known the ways

To remember our pact

With the Maker of days.

I call forth the angels, the courage to bare

And remind of the pure will

In heart we all share.

I call forth the angels the strength of the light

To cast off the shadows

Of the clouds in the night.

I call forth the angels to hold your sweet heart

As you rise to remember.......

This play, and your part.

fusion

Tinsel flames of infinite starlight
Glitter dance static alive in my head
Fireful thoughts of sweet sacred whispers
Sparking in sync through an infinite bed

Light falls upon primordial oceans
Elements sacred Gaia's living delight
Swirling divine expectant rapture
Land's giving birth to the light via night

Sound rises birth through the cape of the cosmos
Will of Love pulses thru chords of design
An infinite moment on one sacred backdrop
Orchestra of the One infinite mind

Rise song of this day on the shores of life's ocean
One cosmic rapture ecstatic in dance
Templates of perfection in One master template
Paired one with All One enlivened enhanced

New is the dawning this day of One order
Harmonic rainbows sing showers of praise
Between golden crystals of a new found foundation
Awaiting the call of a consciousness raised

Star-scripted melodies swim in this ocean
Starlight that flows thru heart-crown of One grand
Harmonious current, living tones, song and singer
Melodies sweetened by Love's ensured plan

Life thus gives life in the heart of the cosmos
Pulsing Its tunes through the stars and the sands
Pristine strings play the song and sweet is the chorus
Song alive in the being – the symphony of Man

Witness ye One-All Creator's ideal song
Instruments crystal, co creating design
Cuelessly timed with the will of the Maker
Rejoicing in chorus their Being Divine

Play down upon me hand of the One God
Sooth my heart with the hum of Your hand
A touch at once gentle yet hurdled with power
Tuning in one stroke the Grand Maker's plan

One song is this song
All one in one chorus
One song is this song
The song THAT I AM.

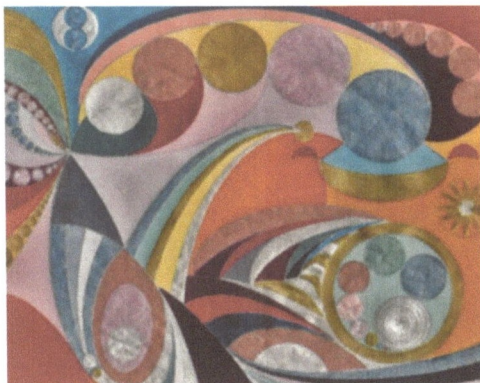

II

SONGS
OF
A NEW DAY

new day

Sacred words my lips do speak,
Sacred songs my heart does beat,
Sacred fire burns my breast,
As sacred waves swirl through my chest.

My tears have flowed upon my cheek
My sadness smothered life to weak
My cries for justice echoed deep
Alone my heart did solemn weep.

Yet now a strange and vibrant beat
Does tickle all my cells to seek,
A vague remembrance cast in light,
That one day life would be aright.

It is the dawn of such a morn
Thru tears of sadness, freshness borne
A life that teams with fragrant hues
And passions fill - reborn anew.

Many are Creators ways
To rattle sleepers hazy gaze
Careful blossom, each sweet petal
Rise to heat on sacred metal.

Solid structure, womb of pain,
Whose power melts by loves refrain,
Let birth begin a flight with wings,
In lands and airs where angels sing.

No more are thoughts of fixed foul states
The makers of my future fate.
A light divine now shines within.
A cosmic smile. A celestial grin.

For as I look afar in gaze
The light I see is brethren raised
The light is yours, and through you shines
Divine - your nature, love sublime.

Let now torrents of ecstasy flow
From One, through all who seek to know.
Rise in One heart, hymn of praise
Let all begin - the new of days.

In silence...

An essence washed through me
Known vague remembrance
To be the essence
Indeed I Am

Coursing through vessels
Of my true nature
Tickling awake the cells and structures
Which delightfully dance as I Am

Pour forth, oh ecstatic current
Live pulsing waves of celestial fondness
Daring to re order
The divine universe of my being

Open my heart
To your timely arrival
Calling me home from the brink
Of forgotten despair

Know, I Am
That which so fondly rekindles -
Love and life's power
One and the same

Flood upon and through
Riverbeds of my presence
Scintillating wash of the shadows
Of a long forgotten dream

I Am That I Am
Indeed One and All
May the currents of the Sun rise
Bless all lighted in the way

A new day is upon us
A daring new beginning
Created by the pulse
Of life's unending flow

Awake ye oh sleeper
Arise from the mists
Which make hazy the journey
From and to the unknown

Silence and Stillness
Key to the floodgates
the blessings of Angels
In the Creator's hand.

Seeds of Starlight

From a place in the sky I could see a great land
As green as an emerald yet blue and so grand.
Intriguing a place as I've seen far and wide,
'Come visit and love me', she sullenly cried.

The voice of an angel appeasing and sweet,
Yet tired, and hopeful we'd once again meet.
The call of this damsel did pierce through my heart
So I flew through the vapors, a seed become dart.

To arrive in the bosom of a being so dressed
I passed through the womb of a child in her breast.
Uncertain of customs and ways of her state
I knew I must wait to continue my fate.

Mask formed in position observing the dream
Sifting thru wisdom experience gleamed,
A wisdom sieved of joy and through fury,
A passage whose constant companion was worry.

I put foot in the ocean of swells on the land
From emotion which rolled among woman and man.
The turbulence caught me like slip in a storm
And threatened to tear every limb from my form.

I raised up my kite to fly in her winds
As thoughts flew around with no destiny pinned,
Planning a future as few owned the land,
The rest then left scattered, as part of no plan.

I cried up to heaven to leave hell of this place,
For I knew that the cosmos was riddled with grace.
A reply quick arrived in her chariot of fire,
In carriage, the true plan - my cry of desire.

It bridled my mind with a force of creation.
It cupped round my heart to give rise to a nation.
It stroked on my cheek in the gift of feather,
And it braced round my spine for the inclement weather.

So I stood there awaiting my grace to depart,
As the plan dare reveal one of Creator's art.
Signs danced, symbols flashed all through the sky,
As the echoes shook loose all the tales to tell why.

The thought of once leaving stood sullenly dim,
My heart filled with joy, cup filled to the brim.
It flowed all around me, into space and to land,
And I suddenly knew that my heart had a plan.

The roots of this love wove deep into the sands.
The leaves of a new tree of life raised their hands,
To gather the sun rays that fall upon form,
Of a jewel in the sea of the cosmos adorned.

Had then I known of the fabulous fate
I know I'd have cried while the treasure did wait.
I praise the sweet wisdom, the love of my soul,
To have veiled the sweet beauty of life, in my role.

Infinite wisdom is part of the script.
Infinite love shall repair any rift.
Infinite grace is the gift of creation.
Infinite power to rise up One nation.

These are cries of the Mother of Sons,
And the children who live as the forsaken ones.
Arise now from sleep and hold open your heart,
As the veils of illusion of death burn apart.

It's time for the fear of the living to die,
To find its own death, as the Son fills the sky,
 And reveals what for time that is known has been planned,
As the hands, that hold time, melt down into the land.

Now is the moment and will always be,
When the joy of creation will dance in the sea,
And the gifts of the mother shall be honored as right,
And eyes rise from illusion to the sweet light of life.

The birth of a star is solemn affair
That sings forth the praises which now fill the air.
A star is now born in a glimmer, a spark,
A star that shall rise in your breast, as your heart.

Such is the tale to be told in the land
When the children of children all dance hand in hand.
The tales they will tell will astound one and all,
As the seeds of the stars rose on high in one call.

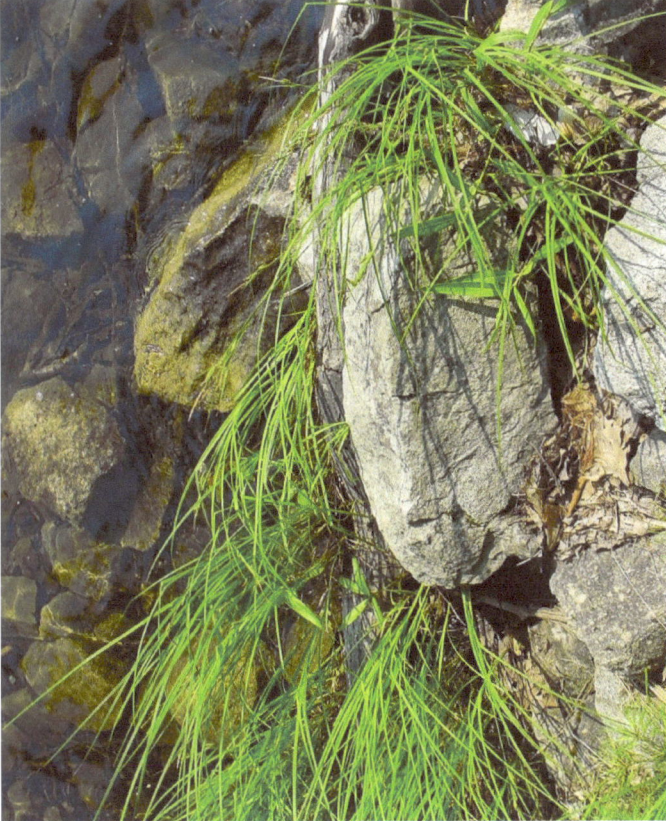

III

SONGS
OF
MODERN NATURE

DELICIOUS SONG

Delicious song
A   dew   filled   morn,
Nourishing deep into the flesh
A   tender   mother's   sleepy   rise.
Sweet caps of love do flesh adorn,
Nature's kiss a dew filled morn.

Symphonic grace does fill the sky,
Light   parades   across   the   crests,
A   caring   mother's   day   begins.
Lightly cease to marvel why
The waltz of life does fill the sky.

The sleepy grace of high noon sun,
With spirits high above the land,
Most   sleep   in   waking   reverie
To   dance   alive   sweet   spirits   fun
Called   forth   through the   high   noon   sun.

The   aft   of   noon   does   settle   near.
The rivers juggles vibrant joys
Which tease my soul in   hymns of praise.
Its   ears   are   those   which   oft   sweet hear
The evening fall does settle near.

The rise of moon
A lullaby
That sings my soul to far off lands,
Chests   of   jewels   in   parallel   space
To   this   days   sacred   ornaments.
Décor   of   a   magic   sigh,
Rising moon sings lullaby.

Chant of peace rise full
The   crickets   sing   in   melody.
Sleepy woods do rest their head,
As   I   rest   my   mine   this   day   of   grace.
Chant   hymns of peace
To fill
this space.

18

So Cycle...

A summer's dream of winter wonder
A winter's praise of summer splendor

A springtime dream of fallen leaves
An autumn sigh for life spring heaves

From winter crusted frozen capes
To roses o'er a summer scape

Or fresh sweet grass,
Never broken
All sweet life
A cosmic token

The swings of cycles far and near
Reflect the smile of grander year

A smile upon Creators face
That smiles upon all mankind race

Let the cycles sing the praise
Hand and heart let mankind raise

The cycles rise to spin anew
An octave fearless
From love
grew.

modern wind

The beauty of whistling wind
Riding waves of solar flight,
A testament of nature's grin,
A heavy heart returns to light.

Such is the kiss of a kind father's blessings,
Such is the lullaby my mother does sing,
Light forms the gift of nature's caressing
To hold now my heart, so its joy will loud ring.

When as a child I awed at your whimsy,
So as a man, I forgot what I knew
To the mutated tokens of a great life, now flimsy.
The longing, a child's heart, emerged as I grew.

I reached to the sky cap, and beyond the heavens
Which to me as child seemed finite though grand.
And I pierced through the clouds with a call of an amend
A wind then blew forth from the gest of a hand.

This is the wind that now I do speak of
This is the breeze that sooths my child ways,
Covering sores that cry for the sweet salve -
Of the Maker of landscapes, the Maker of days.

There is no gust in the land that could scare me.
There is no wave in the sea that wrought fright.
The wave and the breeze are now tempered by your love
As I stand and awaken from the dreams of the night.

This breeze is the grace that answers my beckon,
The wings of an angel that lights at my side.
To grace I give praise for its beauty astounds one
Who fearfully wondered, who'ld weather the ride.

Pull down your bonnet when the wind rises fiercely.
Bare the strands of your wisdom when peace is on land.
Life up your cheeks to the angels of mercy,
When the breath of creation is stirred by God's hand.

Such is the prayer I sing to the heaven.
Such is the song of the wind on the sea.
Such is the call I raise to my brethren
In the breeze of a sweet wind, the blessings will be.

The beauty of a whistling wind
Riding waves of solar flight,
A testament of nature's grin,
A heavy heart returns to light .

CARESS

I long to feel the sway of your sweet caress
In the fabric of my beingness.
I long to swoon in the melodies
Of your celestial song,
Om Maker.

To know of the works of your cosmic fantasies,
Does tantalize me as one with You...
Above the lands of compare.
The song of a chorus known without thinking
Your om shanti shanti ... praise sings.

Where o where are the vibrations, to sooth o'er
My turbulent makings in thought and in deed.
I know your love is beyond compare.
I leave my twisted teardrops at the crossroads
Of your delightful grounds.

Make me a channel of your divine wonder.
Fill me with the ecstasy of divine rapture,
Sweet resonance of your soothing caress.
Yes I do long to be touched once again
As I turn to face your heart.

Is your heart the one that beats my breast?
That fills my longing with one way to turn...
Right back to the Nameless Visage
Of galaxies of dreams.

Surely I long not in vain,
Time is short, as it accelerates
Into the portal of your embrace...
My journey home
... Into your arms.

IV

SONGS
OF
YOU

YOU

The world of form does breath a sigh
As trickles of quaint grandeur
Flow in her veins
Gently releasing the tensions and sorrows
Of a world gripped in fear's promise.

Hark to the chorus of star songs
Whose chants of harmony reminisce
A bygone future of endless delight
As the dance of ages falls solemnly
Upon the heels of the eternal now.

It has been sung by man and woman
Since before the beginning of time
Love's promise
Hark the tune for it rings now in the ears
Of nature's infinite beauty.

I shall not speak of love
And debase its magnificent aura
In a shroud of words that veil its caress
In a promise sadly missed
Through the veils of many guises.

I shall speak instead of you
For you are indeed one and the same
With all love
Then you know with doubt effaced
The living word that flows in the veins of yourself.

Hear the beat of the divine chorus
Fall sweetly into its ecstatic rhythm
Beating from the heart of hearts.
Emerge in the Christening
Of an ancient brave new world.

In You, I Am

Dewdrops of golden nectar
Nestle my heart
From the golden sun

High noon's praises
Caress the silvery strings
Of midnight's embrace

Swirling through space
At infinite speed
In a divine dance

Such are my thoughts
In You.

Cosmic symphony
Chords and carols
Of endless delight

The breath of an angels wing
Tones the fibers
Of my heart strings

As I long to lose myself
In the blissful torrent
Of your divine dreams

Such are my thoughts
In You.

My thoughts are thus
Your thoughts.

My dreams are thus
Your dreams.

My love is thus
Your love.
I am, that I am, in you.

convergence

Vibrations of pure love emit from a blossom,
A tune of proportions, both cosmic and man.
A flower that sits in the breast of my being,
Delightfully poised in the breast of One grand.

I am a cell in the heart of One greater.
I am a bud in the garden of life.
I am a dream, in the mind of the Maker,
Bridegroom and sweet bride, husband and wife.

Who shall try know this who from among you?
Look in a mirror stripped vanity pure,
Through the fog of false reason, I dare you see through it.
A light lifts the mists off insanity's cure.

Know the sweet fragrance my reason for being.
Know the sweet songs the blossoms do sing.
Know the voices that tell of what nature is seeing,
Open your mind into harmony's ring.

Cast off the shells of foul fear's demeanor.
Lift up the pyre of Love's pure intent.
Rise high the swells do the Light of a dreamer,
Flow forth the fragrance the One Heart has sent.

You are cell in the heart of One greater.
You are a bud in the garden of life.
You are at once the dream and the dreamer.
Go now and dream forth One life without strife.

Open your heart and release the sweet fragrance,
Open your mind to dream a new land.
Lamb lie with lion, sweet queen and vagrant
Stripped of the castings, now walk hand in hand.

Rise now the vibrations of an earth rising newness.
Rise now the waters through leaf and through skin.
Rise now the life that quickens the hueless,
The octave converges - rise one and all men.

V

ECSTATIC
FREEDOM TUNES

YES

I long to fill your heart with the ecstasy of mine
To flow thru the hallowed vessel
Burning the tangled webs of imagined isolation
From the corridors of time.

For an instant, while you read,
Let go of your imagined worries -
And feel.

Feel the faint whispers that pulse
Slightly beyond the perceptions of everyday being
But not beyond your imagination.

Your imagination you suppose
For surely this is not hurtful enough to be real.
All that is real is the prickle of a cactus
Or the blunt rage of a world
Recognizing its own madness -
At last!

The time is NOW
And has always been so
It too shall always be
When the memory which beats
The very sinews of your body
Into being …

Would remind you truly
Who I AM.

I speak in speckled verse
To crackle the concepts of imagined wisdom.
For I can not shine through the veils
Put before
The love of My Being,
Your being...In My Being.

I AM not a being
I AM BEING!

As you be
So I am.

Do you remember? Do you dare know?
Where is your courage?
The tenderness of your grace?
I see your strength hiding in the recesses of silly silly fear.
You can not hide forever, from the beauty of your being.

You see.
As I told you,
you are
as
I AM.

free

Long are the tendrils of corridors
Traversing spaces
You are the guest
Guided by worry
Seeking, for an infinite light.

Space and time are the backdrop
As souls lost in unknowing
Peruse hallways of shadows
That disappear as quickly
As they are made real.

Know you are the maker
You indeed are the light

Dancing in projections of thought
Long forgotten in making
Removed by illusion from an imagination
That agreed to make them home.

What is sought in the passage
Gently stands beside you
Gracefully awaiting your call
Waiting to stir the waters of your being
Into living awareness...

Dance...
Dream...

Unshackle your heart from mind's occupied rhetoric
That tickles your heart -- While shackling it in chains!

Let go of the strings
That caress the tenderness, the strength of your being
Let the pulse of life break the bonds
That dare to confuse your precious way.

Be still ... One moment in eternity

Allow the kiss of a moment of presence to remind you

For one eternal moment...
You are free...

unbridle

Let the heat of my heart
Melt swords made of steel.
Let tears of sadness
Blossom roses in modern fields of war.

Let go of false struggles,
Shadows made real.
Awaken to the new divine memory
Fertile seeds planted once not long ago...

Ancient and modern
One time in no time
When the wish of One wish
Not tainted did glow.

Remember your longing
All but forgotten
Now stretched to the brink
Of hope filled despair...

Know of this moment
When winds of the One sun
Would clear away mists
From fields hazy, once fair.

Let go of the thoughts
That divide you from my heart.
It is only one heart
My one heart
You share.

Free flow

Hasten ye now to loosen the purse strings
That clench 'pon the heart
And seal o'er the veil

Open yourself to flow of divine love
Forever your purse shall be filled
With riches of unfathomable beauty and grace

Be humble of mind and
Not in mind
Such are the ways to become your knowing

There is nothing to keep
Worthy of a second regard
In the tensions of your worries

Be humble before the majesty of the Maker
But not in the ideas of your worth
For that is majestic aligned

You shall not find treasure in the pittance of your ideas
Which form frames around you
And keep you in the hurtful folly of forgotten dreams

You are beyond your thoughts in beauty
And they now serve to bind you in the shadow of light
Demand release from the binds of your own thought field

Live once again anew
God is your greatest admirer

In you it is seen the greatest of his works
Struggling in perceived imperfections which are but thoughts
On a silver screen

Remember your beauty in the depth of your heart
Remember indeed who you are
I AM.

37

Hark

Silence the stirs, in the airs, that do crown you.
Silence the waves that flow in your sea.
Rest now and join me in play for a moment.
I hear a faint sound I do pray you join me.

Over the distance a tremble arises,
Not over land but from vistas in space,
While at the same time it echoes from caverns,
I pray you do listen for I hear tunes of grace.

Hark now and listen it's the call of a trumpet!
Bow now your heads while ears span the sky,
Listen between every breath of the cosmos
The first memory of a new sound passes by.

Yet pass by it does not, for it passes right thru us,
And before it expires it sets tune the land,
And though as it passes it seems to expire,
Forever anew is the heart touched of man.

Listen with ears that your head does know not of,
Listen with ears that live deep in space,
For they are the ears that can hear of the chorus,
Do hear, I pray you, time passes by grace.

VI

ONLY
ONE

Only ...

If only I knew of the rays of my being
As child when I looked at the world I was seeing.

If only I heard swells of angels so fair
When as child I oft lis'n to waves in the air.

If only I felt the brush of such grace
When as child my hands reached into sky sacred space.

If only I tasted sweet love that pours down
When as child my lips curled, down into a frown.

If only I smelled the fragrance divine
When as child my nose dipped in the vapors sublime.

If only I remembered the sprays of these rays
When as child I knew well of the Maker of days.

I would never have lived
One lone moment apart
From the love that flows forth
From the harp of one heart.

ABOUT THE AUTHOR

John Ryan is a physician, consciousness and energy based healer, founder of Unity Field Healing and author of The Missing Pill. This collection of poems is his first volume of inspired poetry - shared simply to lift the soul.

www.drjohnryan.org

www.ingramcontent.com/pod-product-compliance
Lightning Source LLC
LaVergne TN
LVHW010023070426
835508LV00001B/25